The
SINGER
and the
SCIENTIST

To my mother the history lover — L.R.

KAR-BEN PUBLISHING, INC.
An imprint of Lerner Publishing Group, Inc.
241 First Avenue North
Minneapolis, MN 55401 USA
1-800-4-KARBEN

Website address: www.karben.com

Main body text set in Cantonia MT Std.
Typeface provided by Monotype Typography.

Photos courtesy of the Library of Congress, p. 32.

Library of Congress Cataloging-in-Publication Data

Names: Rose, Lisa, author. | Muñoz, Isabel, illustrator.
Title: The singer and the scientist / by Lisa Rose ; illustrations by Isabel Muñoz.
Description: Minneapolis : Kar -Ben Publishing, 2021. | Includes bibliographical references. | Audience: Ages 5–11 | Audience: Grades 2–3 | Summary: "Singer Marian Anderson and scientist Albert Einstein become friends, connecting over similar experiences with prejudice and a shared passion for music, when Marian is turned away from a hotel that bars African Americans in mid-century America"— Provided by publisher.
Identifiers: LCCN 2020014827 (print) | LCCN 2020014828 (ebook) | ISBN 9781541576094 (library binding) | ISBN 9781541576100 (paperback) | ISBN 9781728417578 (ebook)
Subjects: LCSH: Anderson, Marian, 1897–1993—Juvenile literature. | Contraltos—United States—Biography—Juvenile literature. | African American singers—Biography—Juvenile literature. | Anderson, Marian, 1897–1993—Friends and associates—Juvenile literature. | Einstein, Albert, 1879–1955—Friends and associates—Juvenile literature.
Classification: LCC ML3930.A5 R67 2021 (print) | LCC ML3930.A5 (ebook) | DDC 782.0092 [B]—dc23

LC record available at https://lccn.loc.gov/2020014827
LC ebook record available at https://lccn.loc.gov/2020014828

Manufactured in the United States of America
1-46598-47603-7/14/2020

The SINGER and the SCIENTIST

by Lisa Rose

illustrated by Isabel Muñoz

KAR-BEN
PUBLISHING

1937, McCarter Theatre, Princeton, New Jersey.
Peeling back the velvet curtain, Marian peeked out at the chatting audience. Furs, diamonds, and pearls dazzled from the women and perfectly tailored suits blazed on the men. Marian knew how rare it was for a white audience of this size to come hear an African American woman sing.

Marian's heart did its nervous thump, thump, thumpity-thump. Her stomach twisted. How would she be able to—

A stagehand signaled that it was time for her to begin.

Taking a deep breath, Marian swept onto the stage. The lights in the theater dimmed. The audience hushed.

The spotlight shone on Marian. She could not turn
back. Nodding to the pianist, she began softly singing

A man in the front row had wild white hair and wrinkled clothes. His foot tapped perfectly to the rhythm of her song. The rest of the audience swayed to the music.

As she sang, each crescendo swept her fears further away.

All eyes in the audience were on her.
All ears in the audience were tuned in to her.
Holding the last note, she wished that the night
would never end.

The piano stopped. Gracefully, Marian bowed, and the audience erupted in applause.

In the wings of the stage, Marian's body sagged with exhaustion. It had been a very long day. She wanted only to take her shoes off and rest. Picking up her suitcase, she headed to the lobby.

The well-dressed people mingled with one another—but not with her. Nobody came up to Marian to compliment her or to thank her or even to say hello. As so often happened, she felt invisible in the white crowd.

The theater owner rushed past her.
Marian had to shout for him to stop.
He turned and looked annoyed as she asked
him to please arrange a room for her at the nearby
Nassau Inn.

His voice boomed loudly as he explained that the Nassau was a whites-only hotel. All talking in the lobby ceased. Everyone looked at Marian, but not as a star. Not even as a person.

The room began to hum again. Her tears welled up. The people who had just minutes before risen to their feet clapping for her now ignored her.

The man with the wild white hair from the front row stepped toward Marian. Now she recognized him. It was the famous scientist and mathematician Albert Einstein.

Einstein's smile stretched across his face. He raved about her performance.

He went on to say that he thought she might be tired and invited her to stay in his extra room for the night.

Stunned, Marian could barely utter, "Thank you."

Albert picked up her suitcase, and they left the theater together, Marian's heels clicking beside him.

As they walked, Albert told her he was from
Germany. He described how things had become
very difficult for the Jewish people in Europe, and
how he had been forced to leave Germany. He told
her the Nazis had taken his house away from him.
He described how the Nazis had even burned his
book on the theory of relativity at a book burning
in the town square.

Marian could understand how painful this must have been for him. She understood what it meant to be treated as an outsider in one's own country.

A woman waved to Albert from her porch as they passed by. Marian waited as Albert stopped to chat. The woman was thanking Albert for his help with her son's math homework.

Marian couldn't believe what she was hearing. The famous Einstein was helping his neighbor, an African American child, with his math homework.

As they walked on, Albert told Marian how much his mother adored music and how she had signed him up for violin lessons when he was only five. He told her that he fell in love with Mozart's sonatas and that he had almost become a musician instead of a scientist.

Marian was surprised to see that
Albert's home looked just like all the other
houses in the neighborhood. She had
thought it would be grander. He opened
the door and invited her in.

For many hours, Marian and Albert shared funny stories. They had coffee and cake. Then, although it was late, Marian asked Albert whether he still played the violin.

Albert leaped from his seat and returned with his well-worn instrument. Propping it under his chin, he slid the bow across the strings.

The soothing sound of the violin touched Marian and
unleashed a song from deep inside her. As Albert played,
Marian sang, It was the beginning of a friendship that would
last long after that evening.

Years later, when the world had changed, Marian
returned to the McCarter Theatre.
This time, the theater owner greeted her graciously and
asked if he could make a reservation for her at the Nassau
Inn nearby.

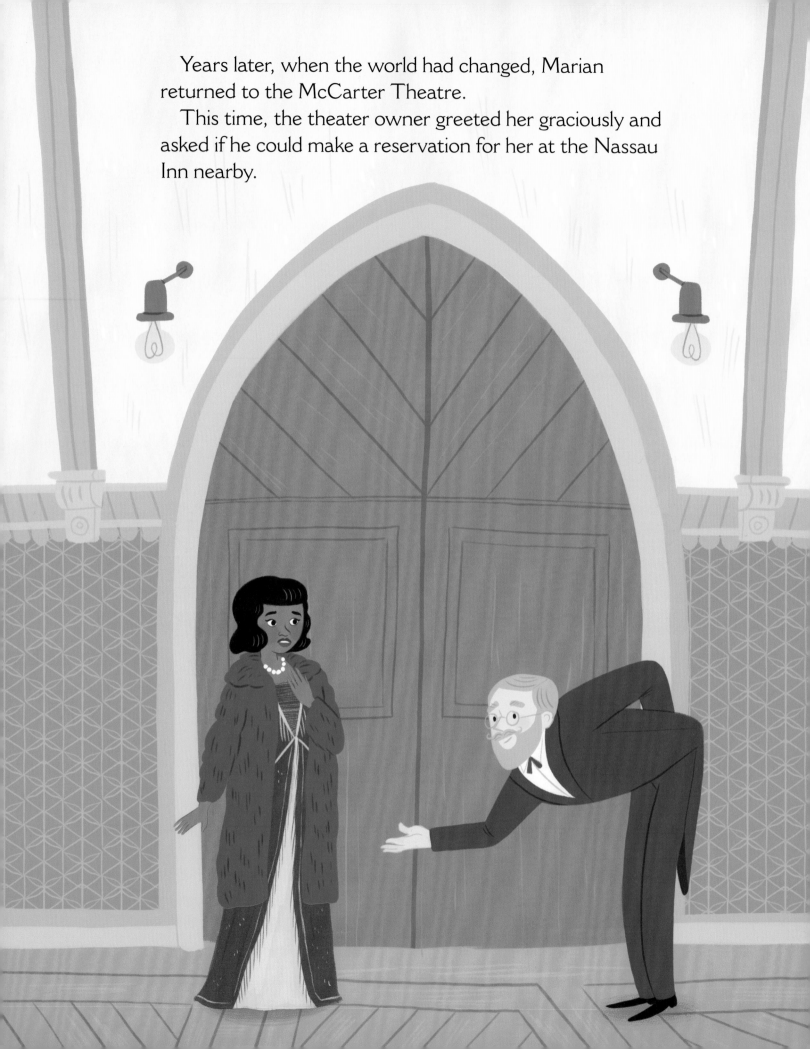

But Marian said, "No, thank you."
She would be staying at the home of her
friend Albert.

Author's Note

Albert Einstein is famous as both a scientist and a mathematician. But he was also a political activist who was interested in the rights of all people. He made speeches, wrote articles, and chaired many organizations urging the end of racism in America.

Marian Anderson was uncomfortable as an activist. Her goal was simply to sing. Her nephew James DePreist wrote, "She saw herself as neither victim nor heroine, simply an artist who happened to be crossing an intersection of United States history when racism collided with conscience."[1]

However, when she began singing in front of segregated audiences, she would bow to the black side of the audience first. Soon, she would quietly decline to sing in front of segregated audiences altogether.

The story of Marian Anderson's performance at the McCarter Theatre in 1937 is not well known. She met Albert Einstein and stayed at his house the night after this event. Her more famous performance came two years later when, in 1939, the Daughters of the American Revolution (DAR) refused to let Marian Anderson sing at Constitution Hall because of her race. Marian was unsurprised. But First Lady Eleanor Roosevelt resigned from the DAR in protest and instead invited Marian Anderson to sing at the Lincoln Memorial on Easter morning. At first, Marian didn't want to go. "I studied my conscience," she wrote in her autobiography. "I could see that my significance as an individual was small in this affair. I had become, whether I liked it or not, a symbol, representing my people. I had to appear."[2] At that concert Marian Anderson sang in front of a multiracial crowd of seventy-five thousand people.

1 Victoria Garrett Jones, *Marian Anderson: A Voice Uplifted* (New York: Sterling, 2008), 76.

2 Marian Anderson, *My Lord, What a Morning: An Autobiography* (New York: Viking, 1956), 189.

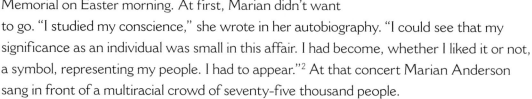
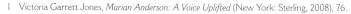